AI-GENERATED DYNAMIC CONTENT FOR DIGITAL ADVERTISING:

CREATE AI ALGORITHMS THAT DYNAMICALLY GENERATE PERSONALIZED AND CONTEXTUALLY RELEVANT CONTENT FOR DIGITAL ADVERTISING, OPTIMIZING AD PERFORMANCE BASED ON REAL-TIME DATA

I0427184

BY

HENRY E. PARKINS

1

COPYRIGHT PAGE

Right reserved, no part of the publication may be republished in any form or by any means, including photo copy, scanning or otherwise without prior written permission to the copyright holder Copyright @2024

HENRY E. PARKINS

TABLE OF CONTENTS

COPYRIGHT PAGE   2

TABLE OF CONTENTS   3

INTRODUCTION   9

Overview of the Current State of Digital Advertising   9

The Role of Personalized and Dynamic Content in Enhancing Ad
Performance   10

The Need for AI-Generated Dynamic Content in the Evolving Digital
Landscape   11

CHAPTER 2   12

AI IN DIGITAL ADVERTISING   12

Exploring the Intersection of AI and Digital Advertising   12

Benefits of Incorporating AI in Content Creation for Ads   13
    Personalization at Scale: 13
    Real-Time Adaptability: 14
    Data-Driven Insights: 14
    Efficiency and Automation: 14

Challenges and Considerations in Implementing AI-Driven Dynamic
Content   15
    Algorithm Bias: 15
    Privacy Concerns: 15
    Resource Intensity: 16
    Transparency and Accountability: 16

3

**Symbiotic Relationship between AI and Digital Advertising, Exploring
How This Fusion Redefines the Very Fabric of Content Creation and
Audience Engagement**   **17**

CHAPTER 3   20

FOUNDATIONS OF AI ALGORITHMS FOR DYNAMIC CONTENT GENERATION   20

Basics of Machine Learning and Natural Language Processing   **20**
Machine Learning Fundamentals: 21
Natural Language Processing Essentials: 21

Training Data Sets and Model Selection for Advertising Content   **22**
Curating Relevant Data Sets: 22
Model Selection for Advertising Content: 22

**Creating Algorithms that Adapt to Real-Time Data for Dynamic
Content Generation**   **23**
Real-Time Data Integration: 23
Dynamic Model Updates: 24
Contextual Content Generation: 24

CHAPTER 4   25

PERSONALIZATION AND CONTEXTUAL RELEVANCE   25

Importance of Personalization in Digital Advertising   **25**
Enhanced User Engagement: 26
Increased Conversion Rates: 26
Brand Loyalty and Retention: 26

Leveraging AI to Understand User Preferences and Behaviors   **26**
Behavioral Analysis: 27
Preference Modeling: 27
Dynamic User Segmentation: 27

**Strategies for Ensuring Contextual Relevance in Dynamically
Generated Content**   **28**
   Real-Time Context Analysis: 28
   Multi-Modal Content Integration: 28
   Dynamic Content Templates: 29
   Geo-Targeted Personalization: 29

CHAPTER 5   30

CASE STUDIES AND SUCCESS STORIES   30

**Examining Successful Implementations of AI-Generated Dynamic
Content**   **30**
   Dynamic Product Recommendations at Scale: 31
   Personalized Email Marketing Campaigns: 31
   Dynamic Banner Ads for Increased Interaction: 31

**Showcase of Notable Brands and Campaigns Utilizing AI for Ad
Personalization**   **32**
   Netflix: Personalized Content Recommendations: 32
   Amazon: AI-Driven Product Recommendations: 32
   Spotify: Dynamic Playlists and Personalized Music
   Recommendations: 33
   Lessons Learned and Best Practices from Real-World Examples: 33
   Data Quality and Diversity: 33
   Iterative Testing and Optimization: 34
   Transparency and Communication: 34

CHAPTER 6   35

ETHICAL CONSIDERATIONS IN AI-GENERATED ADVERTISING CONTENT   35

Navigating Algorithmic Bias and Fairness   **36**
   Understanding Algorithmic Bias: 36

Transparency and User Empowerment   **36**

Transparent Communication Strategies: 36
User Control and Consent: 37

Privacy and Data Security **37**
Respecting User Privacy: 37
Data Security Best Practices: 37

Inclusive and Non-Discriminatory Practices **38**
Ensuring Inclusivity: 38
Mitigating Unintended Consequences: 38

Continuous Ethical Review and Adaptation **38**
Iterative Ethical Evaluation: 38
Industry Collaboration for Ethical Standards: 39

CHAPTER 8 **39**

IMPLEMENTATION STRATEGIES **39**

**Steps to Integrate AI-Generated Dynamic Content into Existing
Advertising Workflows** **40**
Assessment of Current Workflow: 40
Alignment with Business Objectives: 40
Data Infrastructure and Accessibility: 41
Selection of AI Models and Tools: 41

Collaborating with AI Developers and Data Scientists **42**
Interdisciplinary Collaboration: 42
Defining Roles and Responsibilities: 42
Continuous Communication: 42

Scaling AI Implementations for Various Advertising Platforms **43**
Platform Compatibility Assessment: 43
Customization for Different Platforms: 43
Cross-Platform Consistency: 44
Monitoring and Optimization Across Platforms: 44

CHAPTER 9 **45**

FUTURE TRENDS AND INNOVATIONS   45

Emerging Technologies Shaping the Future of AI in Digital Advertising
                                                    45
Advanced Natural Language Processing (NLP):   45
Computer Vision and Visual Content Generation: 46
Conversational AI for Interactive Advertising: 46
Augmented Reality (AR) and Virtual Reality (VR):   46

Predictions for the Evolution of Dynamic Content Generation   **47**
Hyper-Personalization and Individualization: 47
Predictive Content Generation: 47
Dynamic Storytelling: 48
Multimodal Content Fusion: 48

Potential Challenges and Opportunities in the Coming Years   **48**
Privacy and Ethical Considerations: 48
Regulatory Landscape: 49
Data Security and Trust: 49
Integration with Emerging Technologies: 49
AI Literacy and Skill Development: 49

CHAPTER 10   50

CONCLUSION   50

Recap of Key Insights and Takeaways   **51**
Transformation of Digital Advertising: 51
Foundations of AI Algorithms: 51
Personalization and Contextual Relevance: 51
Ethical Considerations: 52
Implementation Strategies: 52

**Encouraging the Adoption of AI-Generated Dynamic Content in
Digital Advertising**   **53**
Embracing Innovation: 53
Investment in Talent and Technology: 53
Educational Initiatives: 53

7

Looking Ahead to the Future of Personalized and Contextually Relevant Ads   **54**

    Continuous Evolution of AI Technologies: 54
    User-Centric Experiences: 54
    Ethical and Responsible Practices: 55
    Global Standardization and Collaboration: 55

Other books by the author   **56**

INTRODUCTION

In the fast-paced realm of digital advertising, staying ahead of the curve is not merely a desire but a necessity. As businesses navigate the ever-evolving landscape of online marketing, the significance of delivering compelling and relevant content to target audiences has become increasingly paramount. The current state of digital advertising is marked by a surge in competition, shifting consumer behaviors, and a growing demand for personalized interactions. To address these challenges and capitalize on opportunities, a groundbreaking paradigm is emerging the integration of artificial intelligence (AI) into the heart of content creation.

Overview of the Current State of Digital Advertising

Digital advertising has witnessed a seismic shift in recent years, propelled by technological advancements and changing consumer expectations. Traditional, static

9

content no longer suffices to capture the attention and loyalty of the modern digital audience. Advertisers find themselves grappling with the need to create more engaging, personalized, and contextually relevant content that resonates with individuals in a meaningful way. This challenge, however, is met with unprecedented opportunities through the harnessing of AI technologies.

The Role of Personalized and Dynamic Content in Enhancing Ad Performance

In a world inundated with information, generic advertising messages often fall flat. Consumers now expect tailored experiences that cater to their preferences, interests, and immediate needs. The power of personalized and dynamic content lies in its ability to go beyond a one-size-fits-all approach. Advertisements that adapt in real-time to user behavior and contextual cues not only capture attention but also foster a deeper connection between brands and their

10

audiences. As we delve into this book, we will explore how AI-generated dynamic content serves as a catalyst for elevating ad performance to unprecedented levels.

The Need for AI-Generated Dynamic Content in the Evolving Digital Landscape

As the digital landscape evolves, so do the expectations of consumers. The era of static, unchanging advertising content is giving way to a dynamic and responsive approach. AI stands at the forefront of this transformation, offering the capability to create content that evolves in sync with the ever-changing digital environment. From adapting to user preferences to optimizing content based on real-time data, AI-generated dynamic content not only addresses the needs of the current digital landscape but propels businesses into the forefront of innovation and relevance.

CHAPTER 1

AI IN DIGITAL ADVERTISING

Exploring the Intersection of AI and Digital Advertising

In the intricate dance of algorithms and consumer engagement, the intersection of artificial intelligence (AI) and digital advertising marks a pivotal moment in the evolution of marketing strategies. AI, with its ability to process vast amounts of data and adapt in real-time, has become a linchpin in crafting personalized and dynamic content that resonates with target audiences. This chapter delves into the symbiotic relationship between AI and digital advertising, exploring how this fusion redefines the very fabric of content creation and audience engagement.

As we dissect the core components of AI, from machine learning to natural language

12

processing, we unravel the potential for these technologies to revolutionize the way advertisers connect with consumers. By understanding the underlying mechanisms, we empower ourselves to harness the true capabilities of AI in crafting content that not only captures attention but also builds lasting relationships with users.

Benefits of Incorporating AI in Content Creation for Ads

The incorporation of AI in content creation transcends mere novelty; it is a strategic imperative for businesses seeking to thrive in the dynamic landscape of digital advertising. This section explores the myriad benefits that arise from marrying AI with advertising creativity:

Personalization at Scale: AI enables advertisers to move beyond demographic targeting and create personalized content at scale. By analyzing user behavior, preferences, and historical data, AI algorithms dynamically tailor content to match individual interests,

ensuring a more meaningful connection with the audience.

Real-Time Adaptability: In the ever-changing digital ecosystem, relevance is paramount. AI empowers advertisers to create content that adapts in real-time to shifts in user behavior, market trends, and contextual cues. This nimbleness enhances the likelihood of capturing user attention and driving engagement.

Data-Driven Insights: AI algorithms process vast datasets, extracting actionable insights that inform content creation strategies. By understanding user patterns and preferences, advertisers can make informed decisions, optimizing campaigns for better performance and return on investment.

Efficiency and Automation: AI streamlines the content creation process by automating tasks that would be time-consuming for humans. This efficiency allows advertisers to focus on strategy and creativity while AI handles repetitive tasks, leading to increased productivity.

14

Challenges and Considerations in Implementing AI-Driven Dynamic Content

While the benefits are substantial, the integration of AI-driven dynamic content into digital advertising is not without its challenges and considerations. Navigating the following aspects is crucial for a successful implementation:

Algorithm Bias:

The risk of perpetuating biases present in training data is a significant concern. Advertisers must carefully monitor and address biases in AI algorithms to ensure fair and inclusive content generation.

Privacy Concerns:

The collection and utilization of user data for personalized content raise privacy considerations. Striking a balance between personalization and respecting user privacy is imperative to build trust and comply with regulations.

Resource Intensity: Implementing AI-driven dynamic content requires significant resources, including skilled personnel, computing power, and robust infrastructure. Advertisers must carefully assess and allocate resources to avoid potential bottlenecks.

Transparency and Accountability: As AI autonomously generates content, ensuring transparency in the decision-making process becomes challenging. Advertisers must strive for transparency and establish accountability mechanisms to maintain trust with users and stakeholders.

Symbiotic Relationship between AI and Digital Advertising, Exploring How This Fusion Redefines the Very Fabric of Content Creation and Audience Engagement

The symbiotic relationship between AI and digital advertising represents a transformative union that reshapes the landscape of content creation and audience engagement. This fusion goes beyond mere technological integration; it establishes a dynamic partnership where AI becomes the catalyst for unprecedented levels of innovation and effectiveness in digital marketing.

In the realm of content creation, AI acts as a creative collaborator, augmenting human ingenuity with its ability to process vast amounts of data at unparalleled speeds. This collaboration extends the boundaries of what is possible, enabling marketers to move beyond static, one-size-fits-all

17

approaches. By analyzing user behaviors, preferences, and interactions, AI unlocks a treasure trove of insights that inform the creation of personalized and contextually relevant content.

At the core of this symbiosis is the capacity of AI to adapt in real-time. The dynamic nature of the digital landscape demands content that is not only tailored to individual preferences but also responsive to shifts in market trends and user behaviors. AI algorithms continuously learn and evolve, ensuring that the content they generate remains aligned with the ever-changing interests of the audience. This adaptability not only enhances the relevance of content but also ensures that brands stay agile in the face of a rapidly evolving digital ecosystem.

Moreover, the symbiotic relationship between AI and digital advertising extends its influence to audience engagement. AI-driven content, crafted with a deep understanding of individual preferences, captures attention more effectively. By delivering personalized experiences, advertisers foster a sense of connection and resonance with users, transcending

18

the limitations of generic messaging. This heightened engagement, in turn, fuels brand loyalty and encourages meaningful interactions between consumers and brands.

As this symbiosis continues to evolve, it catalyzes a paradigm shift in the very fabric of digital advertising. The traditional boundaries between man and machine blur as AI becomes an integral part of the creative process. The synergy between human creativity and machine intelligence leads to a level of content personalization and contextual relevance that was once unimaginable.

This fusion not only redefines how content is created but also challenges conventional notions of audience engagement. The symbiotic relationship between AI and digital advertising is not just a technological advancement; it is a reimagining of the possibilities inherent in the intersection of data-driven insights and human ingenuity. As we navigate this transformative landscape, the synergy between AI and digital advertising becomes a driving force, propelling the industry into an era where the boundaries

19

of creativity and engagement are continually pushed and redefined.

CHAPTER 2

FOUNDATIONS OF AI ALGORITHMS FOR DYNAMIC CONTENT GENERATION

Basics of Machine Learning and Natural Language Processing

In the intricate tapestry of AI-generated dynamic content for digital advertising, the foundational threads are woven through the basics of machine learning (ML) and natural language processing (NLP). Understanding these fundamental principles is paramount for advertisers seeking to harness the true power of AI in crafting personalized and contextually relevant content.

Machine Learning Fundamentals:

a. Supervised learning, unsupervised learning, and reinforcement learning. b. Feature extraction and representation for advertising data. c. Model training, evaluation, and deployment.

Natural Language Processing Essentials:

a. Tokenization, stemming, and lemmatization for text analysis. b. Named entity recognition and sentiment analysis. c. Language models and embedding for understanding context.

As advertisers delve into the world of machine learning and natural language processing, they gain the tools necessary to extract meaningful insights from data and enable AI algorithms to comprehend and generate content that resonates with the nuances of language and user behavior.

Training Data Sets and Model Selection for Advertising Content

The efficacy of AI-generated dynamic content hinges on the careful selection of training data sets and models tailored to the specific nuances of digital advertising. This section illuminates the critical steps involved in this process.

Curating Relevant Data Sets:

a. Identifying and collecting diverse data sets representing user behaviors. b. Cleaning and preprocessing data to ensure quality and relevance. c. Balancing the data to avoid biases and enhance generalization.

Model Selection for Advertising Content:

a. Understanding the suitability of various machine learning models (e.g., decision trees, neural networks). b. Tailoring models for specific advertising objectives, such as click-through rate optimization or user segmentation. c. Evaluating model performance through metrics like accuracy, precision, and recall.

By aligning training data sets and models with the unique requirements of digital advertising, advertisers pave the way for AI algorithms that can discern patterns, preferences, and context to generate content that speaks directly to the intended audience.

Creating Algorithms that Adapt to Real-Time Data for Dynamic Content Generation

The dynamic nature of the digital landscape necessitates AI algorithms capable of adapting to real-time data, ensuring the relevance and timeliness of the generated content. This section illuminates the principles guiding the creation of such adaptable algorithms:

Real-Time Data Integration:

a. Establishing pipelines for continuous data ingestion. b. Handling and processing real-time data streams. c. Integrating external data sources for comprehensive insights.

Dynamic Model Updates:

a. Implementing algorithms that can be fine-tuned with minimal latency. b. Balancing model stability with the need for rapid adaptation. c. Leveraging techniques such as online learning for continuous improvement.

Contextual Content Generation:

a. Incorporating contextual cues from real-time data into content generation. b. Adapting language models to changing user behaviors and preferences. c. Ensuring that dynamically generated content aligns with current market trends.

As advertisers embrace the foundations of AI algorithms for dynamic content generation, they embark on a journey of continuous improvement and innovation. The ability to adapt to real-time data empowers AI to not only keep pace with the evolving digital landscape but to stay

25

ahead, shaping a future where personalized and contextually relevant content is not just a goal but a dynamic reality.

CHAPTER 3

PERSONALIZATION AND CONTEXTUAL RELEVANCE

Importance of Personalization in Digital Advertising

In the crowded digital landscape, where consumers are bombarded with a plethora of information, personalization emerges as the linchpin of effective advertising strategies. The ability to tailor content to individual preferences and behaviors transforms advertisements from mere static messages into personalized experiences. This section explores the profound significance of personalization in digital advertising:

Enhanced User Engagement:

a. Personalized content captures and maintains user attention. b. Tailored

27

messaging resonates more deeply, fostering a sense of connection.

Increased Conversion Rates:

a. Relevant and personalized content leads to higher conversion rates. b. Users are more likely to take desired actions when content aligns with their interests.

Brand Loyalty and Retention:

a. Personalized experiences contribute to building brand loyalty. b. Consistently relevant content encourages repeat engagement and customer retention.

Leveraging AI to Understand User Preferences and Behaviors

The advent of AI in digital advertising has ushered in a new era where understanding user preferences and behaviors goes beyond surface-level analysis. AI algorithms have the capability to delve deep into data, uncovering intricate patterns and nuances. This section

28

explores the pivotal role of AI in decoding user preferences and behaviors:

Behavioral Analysis:

a. Analyzing user interactions with content to identify patterns. b. Uncovering behavioral trends that inform content customization.

Preference Modeling:

a. Building models that capture individual preferences based on historical data. b. Utilizing machine learning to predict user preferences in real-time.

Dynamic User Segmentation:

a. Employing AI algorithms to dynamically segment users based on current behaviors. b. Creating personalized content for distinct user segments.

Strategies for Ensuring Contextual Relevance in Dynamically Generated Content

Context is the secret sauce that transforms personalized content from merely relevant to compellingly resonant. AI plays a pivotal role in ensuring that dynamically generated content aligns seamlessly with the current context. This section delves into strategies to achieve contextual relevance:

Real-Time Context Analysis:

a. Implementing algorithms that analyze real-time data to understand the current context. b. Adapting content generation based on contextual cues, such as trending topics or events.

Multi-Modal Content Integration:

a. Incorporating diverse content formats based on contextual relevance. b. Utilizing a mix of text, images, and videos to enhance engagement.

30

Dynamic Content Templates:

a. Designing flexible content templates that can be dynamically populated. b. Allowing for variations in messaging based on contextual factors.

Geo-Targeted Personalization:

a. Leveraging location data to customize content based on geographic relevance. b. Tailoring promotions and messages to local trends and preferences.

As advertisers embark on the journey of creating AI-generated dynamic content, the harmonious interplay between personalization and contextual relevance becomes the hallmark of success. By understanding the importance of tailoring content to individual preferences, leveraging AI to decode user behaviors, and implementing strategies for contextual relevance, advertisers unlock the potential to captivate audiences in a way that transcends traditional advertising norms. In the age of AI-driven personalization, advertisements become not just messages

31

but personalized and contextually rich experiences.

CHAPTER 4

CASE STUDIES AND SUCCESS STORIES

Examining Successful Implementations of AI-Generated Dynamic Content

In the dynamic realm of digital advertising, success stories abound when it comes to the implementation of AI-generated dynamic content. This section delves into real-world examples, showcasing instances where the marriage of AI algorithms and dynamic content creation has led to remarkable achievements:

Dynamic Product Recommendations at Scale:

a. Exploration of e-commerce platforms that leverage AI to dynamically recommend products based on user preferences. b. Examination of algorithms that adapt to changing user behaviors, leading to increased click-through rates and conversion.

Personalized Email Marketing Campaigns:

a. Case studies of email marketing campaigns that utilize AI to dynamically tailor content for individual subscribers. b. Analysis of how personalized email content enhances engagement and drives higher open and click-through rates.

Dynamic Banner Ads for Increased Interaction:

a. Showcase of brands using AI to create banner ads that adapt in real-time to user interactions. b. Metrics on improved engagement and conversion rates compared to static banner ads.

Showcase of Notable Brands and Campaigns Utilizing AI for Ad Personalization

Highlighting the pioneers in the field, this section provides a detailed look at notable brands and their successful campaigns that have harnessed the power of AI for ad personalization:

Netflix: Personalized Content Recommendations:

a. Exploration of how Netflix employs AI algorithms to recommend personalized content to millions of users. b. Insights into how this approach enhances user satisfaction and retention.

Amazon: AI-Driven Product Recommendations: a. Analysis of Amazon's use of AI to dynamically recommend products to users based on their browsing and purchase history. b. Examination of the impact on Amazon's revenue and customer satisfaction.

35

Spotify: Dynamic Playlists and Personalized Music Recommendations:

a. Showcase of how Spotify leverages AI to curate dynamic playlists and provide personalized music recommendations. b. Insights into user engagement and the role of AI in shaping the music streaming experience.

Lessons Learned and Best Practices from Real-World Examples:

The success stories and case studies presented in this chapter are not just anecdotes; they offer valuable lessons and best practices for advertisers looking to embark on their AI-driven dynamic content journey:

Data Quality and Diversity:

a. Importance of collecting and maintaining high-quality, diverse data sets for effective AI-driven content generation. b. Lessons on avoiding biases in training data to ensure fair and inclusive advertising.

Iterative Testing and Optimization:

a. Showcase of brands conducting iterative testing and optimization of AI algorithms for continuous improvement. b. Lessons on the significance of monitoring and refining AI models based on real-time performance data.

Transparency and Communication:

a. Examining how successful brands communicate the use of AI in content personalization to build trust with consumers. b. Insights into transparent practices that address privacy concerns and foster positive user experiences.

CHAPTER 5

ETHICAL CONSIDERATIONS IN AI-GENERATED ADVERTISING CONTENT

As the digital advertising landscape embraces the transformative power of AI-generated dynamic content, a parallel discourse emerges one that revolves around the ethical considerations inherent in this intersection of technology and creativity. This chapter delves into the critical ethical dimensions that advertisers must navigate when leveraging AI for content personalization and explores lessons learned and best practices from real-world examples.

Navigating Algorithmic Bias and Fairness

Understanding Algorithmic Bias:

a. Examination of real-world instances where algorithmic bias has influenced AI-generated content. b. Discussion on the ethical implications of biased content in digital advertising.

Addressing Fairness Concerns: a. Showcase of brands implementing measures to identify and mitigate biases in AI algorithms. b. Insights into strategies for ensuring fair and equitable content generation.

Transparency and User Empowerment

Transparent Communication Strategies:

a. Case studies highlighting brands that communicate openly about the use of AI in content personalization. b. Exploration of effective communication strategies that empower users with knowledge about how their data is utilized.

User Control and Consent:

a. Showcase of brands providing users with control over personalized content settings. b. Lessons on obtaining clear and informed consent for data utilization in AI-driven advertising.

Privacy and Data Security

Respecting User Privacy: a. Examination of brands implementing robust privacy measures in AI-driven advertising content. b. Insights into how transparent data collection and utilization practices enhance user trust.

Data Security Best Practices: a. Showcase of notable brands employing state-of-the-art data security measures to protect user information. b. Lessons learned from real-

world examples on safeguarding user data in the era of AI-driven advertising.

Inclusive and Non-Discriminatory Practices

Ensuring Inclusivity:

a. Exploration of successful campaigns that prioritize inclusivity in AI-generated content. b. Insights into the importance of diverse representation and avoiding discriminatory practices.

Mitigating Unintended Consequences:

a. Case studies that highlight brands proactively addressing unintended consequences of AI-generated content. b. Lessons on monitoring and adapting algorithms to avoid harm and discrimination.

Continuous Ethical Review and Adaptation

Iterative Ethical Evaluation:

a. Showcase of brands incorporating continuous ethical review processes into their AI-driven content strategies. b. Insights into the importance of adapting ethical considerations as technology evolves.

Industry Collaboration for Ethical Standards:

a. Discussion on collaborative efforts within the industry to establish ethical standards for AI-driven advertising. b. Insights into the role of industry associations and regulatory bodies in shaping ethical practices.

CHAPTER 6

IMPLEMENTATION STRATEGIES

As the promise of AI-generated dynamic content beckons, advertisers must navigate the terrain of implementation strategies to seamlessly integrate these cutting-edge technologies into their existing workflows. This chapter explores the essential steps, collaborative practices, and scaling considerations that pave the way for successful deployment of AI-driven dynamic content in digital advertising.

Steps to Integrate AI-Generated Dynamic Content into Existing Advertising Workflows

Assessment of Current Workflow:

43

a. Conducting a thorough analysis of existing advertising workflows. b. Identifying bottlenecks and opportunities for integration with AI-generated dynamic content.

Alignment with Business Objectives:

a. Clearly defining advertising goals and objectives that align with AI-driven content strategies. b. Ensuring that the integration supports overarching business strategies.

Data Infrastructure and Accessibility:

a. Evaluating the readiness of data infrastructure to support AI algorithms. b. Ensuring accessibility to relevant data sources for training and real-time adaptation.

Selection of AI Models and Tools:

a. Researching and selecting AI models suitable for advertising objectives. b. Evaluating tools and platforms that

44

facilitate seamless integration with existing workflows.

Pilot Testing and Iterative Implementation: a. Implementing AI-generated dynamic content in controlled pilot campaigns. b. Iteratively refining the implementation based on performance feedback and user responses.

Collaborating with AI Developers and Data Scientists

Interdisciplinary Collaboration:

a. Fostering collaboration between advertising teams, AI developers, and data scientists. b. Encouraging cross-functional understanding to bridge communication gaps.

Defining Roles and Responsibilities:

a. Clearly delineating roles and responsibilities within the collaborative

45

team. b. Establishing communication channels for seamless information flow.

Continuous Communication:

a. Implementing regular check-ins and progress updates between advertising and technical teams. b. Addressing challenges and evolving requirements through ongoing communication.

Agile Development Practices: a. embracing agile methodologies to facilitate flexibility and rapid iteration. b. Leveraging sprints and feedback loops to optimize collaboration and project outcomes.

Scaling AI Implementations for Various Advertising Platforms

Platform Compatibility Assessment:

a. Evaluating the compatibility of AI-generated content with diverse advertising platforms. b. Ensuring adherence to

46

platform-specific guidelines and requirements.

Customization for Different Platforms:

a. Adapting AI models and content templates for specific platform nuances. b. Customizing strategies based on the unique characteristics of each advertising channel.

Cross-Platform Consistency:

a. Maintaining a consistent brand message and user experience across multiple platforms. b. Balancing customization with the need for cohesive brand representation.

Monitoring and Optimization across Platforms: a. implementing robust monitoring mechanisms for performance across various platforms. b. Iteratively optimizing strategies based on platform-specific data and insights.

As advertisers embark on the journey of implementing AI-generated dynamic

47

content, a strategic approach that encompasses workflow integration, collaborative practices, and platform scalability is paramount. By following these guidelines, advertisers can not only seamlessly integrate AI technologies but also ensure that the implementation aligns with business objectives, fosters effective collaboration, and scales across diverse advertising platforms, leading to a new era of personalized and contextually relevant digital advertising.

CHAPTER 7

FUTURE TRENDS AND INNOVATIONS

The landscape of digital advertising is in a constant state of evolution, with AI-generated dynamic content standing at the forefront of innovation. This chapter explores the emerging technologies shaping the future, predictions for the evolution of dynamic content generation, and the potential challenges and opportunities that lie ahead in the coming years.

Emerging Technologies Shaping the Future of AI in Digital Advertising

Advanced Natural Language Processing (NLP): a. Exploration of enhanced NLP capabilities for more nuanced understanding of user intent. b. Application of advanced language models

49

for content generation that reflects a deeper understanding of context and sentiment.

Computer Vision and Visual Content Generation:

a. Integration of computer vision technologies for dynamic visual content generation. b. Enhanced capabilities in recognizing and adapting to visual cues, leading to more immersive and engaging ad experiences.

Conversational AI for Interactive Advertising:

a. Leveraging conversational AI to enable interactive and dialog-driven advertising experiences. b. Predictions on the evolution of chatbots and virtual assistants as integral components of dynamic content strategies.

Augmented Reality (AR) and Virtual Reality (VR):

a. Exploration of AI-powered AR and VR applications in advertising. b. Prediction of

50

interactive and immersive ad experiences that blend seamlessly with the real-world environment.

Predictions for the Evolution of Dynamic Content Generation

Hyper-Personalization and Individualization:

a. Prediction of even more sophisticated personalization techniques. b. Hyper-personalization, where content is uniquely tailored to individual preferences and behaviors, becoming a standard practice.

Predictive Content Generation:

a. Exploration of predictive algorithms anticipating user needs before explicit signals. b. Adapting content in anticipation of user behavior, creating a more anticipatory and responsive advertising approach.

Dynamic Storytelling:

51

a. Evolution towards dynamic storytelling approaches. b. Predictions on AI-driven narratives that dynamically adapt based on user engagement and evolving brand narratives.

Multimodal Content Fusion:

a. Integration of diverse content formats in a seamless, multimodal approach. b. Predictions on AI-generated content that combines text, images, audio, and video for a more comprehensive user experience.

Potential Challenges and Opportunities in the Coming Years

Privacy and Ethical Considerations:

a. Potential challenges in balancing personalization with user privacy. b. Opportunities for industry leaders to establish and adhere to ethical standards, fostering trust among users.

Regulatory Landscape:

a. Challenges arising from evolving data protection and privacy regulations. b. Opportunities for advertisers to proactively comply with regulations, enhancing user confidence and avoiding legal complications.

Data Security and Trust:

a. Challenges related to ensuring the security of user data in an increasingly interconnected landscape. b. Opportunities to invest in robust data security measures, building and maintaining user trust.

Integration with Emerging Technologies:

a. Challenges in integrating AI-generated content with rapidly evolving technologies. b. Opportunities for early adopters to leverage emerging technologies for a competitive edge in the advertising space.

AI Literacy and Skill Development:

a. Challenges in fostering AI literacy among marketing professionals. b. Opportunities for training and skill development to empower advertisers in harnessing the full potential of AI-driven dynamic content.

As we gaze into the future of AI-generated dynamic content for digital advertising, the interplay of emerging technologies, predictions for evolution, and the identification of potential challenges and opportunities become critical. Navigating this future landscape requires a strategic vision, a commitment to ethical practices, and a continuous drive for innovation in the dynamic and ever-evolving realm of digital advertising.

54

CHAPTER 8

CONCLUSION

As we conclude this journey through the realm of "AI-Generated Dynamic Content for Digital Advertising," we reflect on the key insights and takeaways that illuminate the path to a new era of advertising creativity and innovation.

Recap of Key Insights and Takeaways

Transformation of Digital Advertising:

a. The shift from static to dynamic content marks a transformative moment in the digital advertising landscape. b. AI emerges as a catalyst, enabling personalized and contextually relevant content at scale.

Foundations of AI Algorithms:

a. Understanding the basics of machine learning and natural language processing is fundamental. b. Training data sets, model selection, and real-time adaptability lay the groundwork for effective AI-driven content creation.

Personalization and Contextual Relevance:

a. Personalization is the cornerstone of engaging advertising experiences. b. The interplay between AI and user behaviors ensures contextually relevant content that resonates with audiences.

Ethical Considerations:

a. Addressing algorithmic bias, ensuring transparency, and respecting user privacy are ethical imperatives. b. Industry collaboration and continuous ethical evaluation are essential for responsible AI-driven advertising.

Implementation Strategies:

a. Integrating AI-generated dynamic content requires a strategic approach. b. Collaboration between advertising teams,

AI developers, and data scientists is crucial for success. c. Scaling AI implementations across various platforms demands customization and cross-platform consistency.

Encouraging the Adoption of AI-Generated Dynamic Content in Digital Advertising

Embracing Innovation:

a. The adoption of AI-generated dynamic content is not just a technological leap but a cultural shift. b. Encouraging a mindset of innovation and adaptability is key to staying at the forefront of advertising trends.

Investment in Talent and Technology:

a. Nurturing talent with expertise in AI and digital advertising is essential. b. Investment in cutting-edge technologies and tools ensures the continual evolution of AI-driven strategies.

57

Educational Initiatives:

a. Promoting awareness and understanding of AI among advertising professionals is critical. b. Educational initiatives and training programs contribute to building a skilled workforce capable of harnessing AI's potential.

Looking Ahead to the Future of Personalized and Contextually Relevant Ads

Continuous Evolution of AI Technologies:

a. The future holds the promise of advanced AI technologies, pushing the boundaries of personalization and context. b. Integration with emerging technologies such as AR, VR, and advanced NLP will redefine the possibilities in dynamic content generation.

User-Centric Experiences:

a. The focus on user-centric experiences will drive the evolution of personalized ads. b. Predictive algorithms, conversational AI, and hyper-personalization will contribute to more meaningful interactions between brands and consumers.

Ethical and Responsible Practices:

a. The future demands a heightened commitment to ethical practices in AI-driven advertising. b. Proactive adherence to privacy regulations, transparent communication, and inclusive strategies will be paramount.

Global Standardization and Collaboration:

a. The industry is poised for global standardization of ethical AI practices. b. Collaboration between businesses, regulatory bodies, and technology developers will shape the responsible evolution of AI in advertising.

In concluding this exploration, we recognize that AI-generated dynamic

59

content is not just a tool; it is a paradigm shift in the way brands connect with their audiences. As we look ahead, the canvas of digital advertising expands, offering a space for creativity, innovation, and a deeper understanding of the diverse and dynamic preferences of users. The future beckons an era where ads are not just messages but personalized and contextually relevant experiences that resonate with individuals in profound ways. As advertisers embark on this journey, the fusion of AI and creativity promises to redefine the very essence of storytelling and engagement in the ever-evolving landscape of digital advertising.

Other books by the author

https://www.amazon.com/author/henryepar
kins

Note Page 5...........................Date................

Use this page for all writing during reading or study.

Note Page 5...........................Date.................

Use this page for all writing during reading or study.

Note Page 5..........................Date................

Use this page for all writing during reading or study.

Note Page 5..........................Date................

Use this page for all writing during reading or study.

Note Page 5...........................Date................

Use this page for all writing during reading or study.

Note Page 5...........................Date................

Use this page for all writing during reading or study.

Note Page 5...........................Date................

Use this page for all writing during reading or study.

Note Page 5..........................Date................

Use this page for all writing during reading or study.

Note Page 5...........................Date................

Use this page for all writing during reading or study.

Note Page 5...........................Date................

Use this page for all writing during reading or study.

Note Page 5..........................Date...............

Use this page for all writing during reading or study.

Note Page 5...........................Date................

Use this page for all writing during reading or study.

Note Page 5............................Date................

Use this page for all writing during reading or study.

Note Page 5...........................Date................

Use this page for all writing during reading or study.

Note Page 5..........................Date...............

Use this page for all writing during reading or study.

Note Page 5...........................Date................

Use this page for all writing during reading or study.

Note Page 5..........................Date................

Use this page for all writing during reading or study.

Note Page 5...........................Date................

Use this page for all writing during reading or study.

Note Page 5..........................Date................

Use this page for all writing during reading or study.

Note Page 5.........................Date...............

Use this page for all writing during reading or study.

Note Page 5..........................Date................

Use this page for all writing during reading or study.

Note Page 5..........................Date................

Use this page for all writing during reading or study.

Note Page 5..........................Date...............

Use this page for all writing during reading or study.

Note Page 5...........................Date................

Use this page for all writing during reading or study.

Note Page 5...........................Date................

Use this page for all writing during reading or study.

www.ingramcontent.com/pod-product-compliance
Lightning Source LLC
Chambersburg PA
CBHW071100290526
45795CB00004B/1589